KAL MASS MEDIA

This platform enables anyone to create cash by implementing
advertising and marketing methods from kalmassmedia.com

Rishi Pal Sharma

Chapters you are going to learn:

- All about Kal Mass Media
- For readers, how can they use?
- Understanding the points
- For author.
- For storyteller
- For students
- For businesses
- For teachers
- For professionals.
- For marketers
- For Journalist.
- EBooks
- Create a free profile.
- Introduce yourself.
- Library program
- Shopping for your daily needs
- Cash your points.
- Affiliate income.
- Conclusion.

As a information researcher for readers and inspiring author to write continues good content. This platform enables anyone to create cash by implementing advertising and marketing methods from kalmassmedia.com.

Let us start our journey to success together.

Kal Mass Media caters to individuals who derive pleasure from both reading and writing. By engaging with current events, you not only broaden your comprehension but also remain informed about popular subjects and recent developments in areas such as business, marketing, health, and social issues. Furthermore, our affiliate scheme enables our customers to gain passive revenue by earning points through activities such as reading, sharing links, and shopping at their preferred businesses in many countries.

Writers have the ability to produce articles, press releases, reviews, essays, revision notes, or fiction. Furthermore, we monitored our users' activities by allocating those points. Authors accumulate points for their publications and receive rewards each time readers engage with the content. These points can be exchanged for monetary compensation, incentives, and further advantages, serving as a strong motivation for writers to persist in providing good content.

Comprehensive information regarding Kal Mass Media Kal Mass Media is a complete platform that enables users to make passive income through many advertising and marketing tactics. This guide aims to provide readers with a comprehensive understanding of how to efficiently employ Kal Mass Media for their individual objectives. Irrespective of whether you are a storyteller, student, business owner, teacher, professional, or marketer, our platform offers significant materials and tools to assist you in accomplishing your objectives. In addition, the guide examines the advantages of establishing a complimentary presence on Kal Mass Media and offers advice on effectively presenting oneself to society for optimal influence. This guide continues by incorporating chapters on library program, shopping for everyday necessities, and redeeming your points for affiliate money. It also extends an invitation to engage in a collective journey towards achievement.

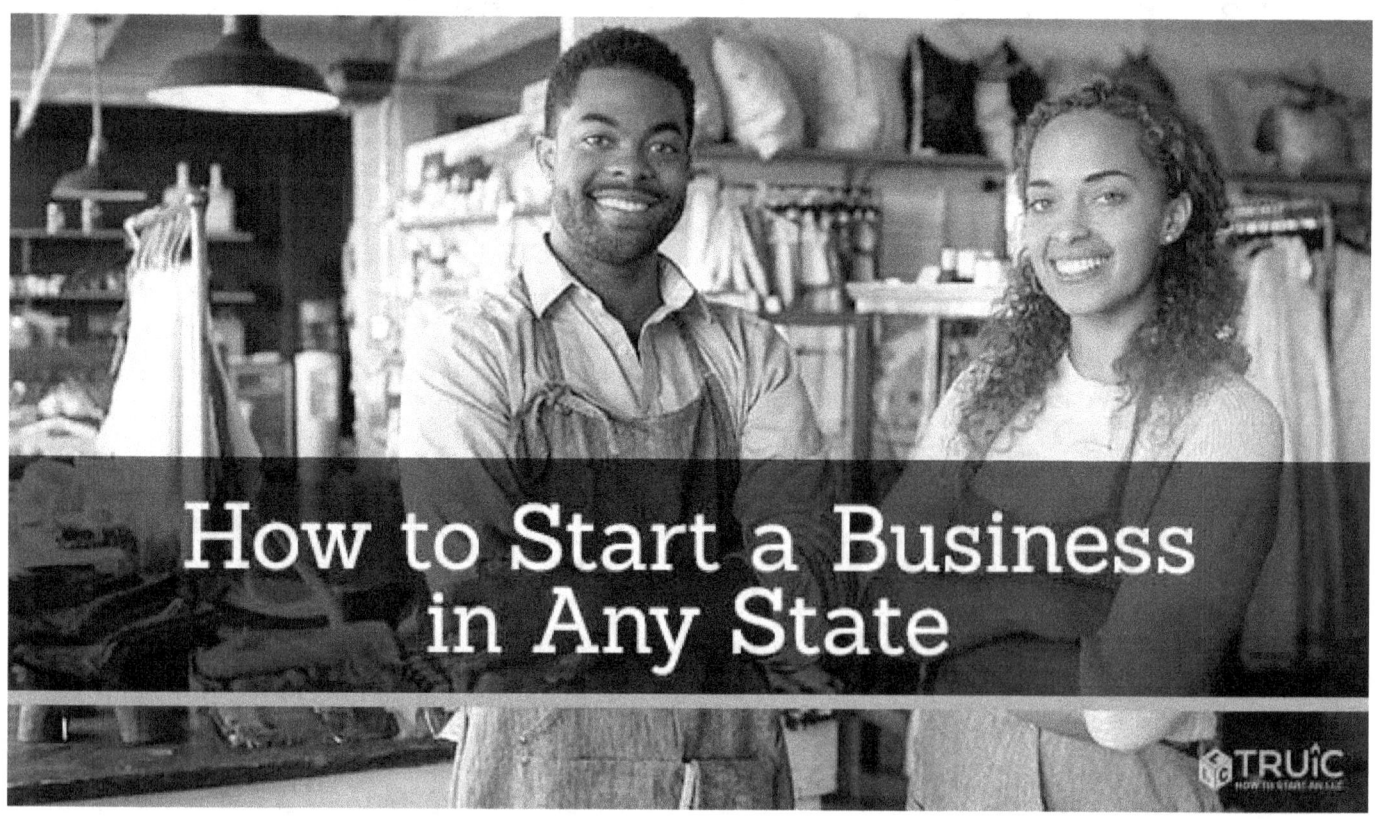

For readers, how can they use?

For readers, they can use our platform to access a wide range of resources, such as tutorials, case studies, and industry insights that are specifically tailored to their needs. Additionally, they can leverage the platform's networking features to connect with like-minded professionals and expand their professional circle. By utilizing these tools and engaging in the collective journey towards achievement, readers can enhance their skills, stay updated with the latest trends, and ultimately achieve their goals in their respective fields. They can also gain valuable insights and knowledge from others in the industry.

Become a free subscriber and enhance your knowledge and income with Kal Mass Media.

Subscribe to our comprehensive database for valuable insights and skills to tackle any challenge with confidence. Stays updated with industry trends and best practices. In addition, enhance your business website's performance, with our informative articles, tutorials, and resources. Our database offers a wide range of valuable insights and skills that will equip you with the necessary tools to confidently tackle any challenge. By subscribing, you will also gain access to the latest industry trends and best practices, ensuring that your business stays ahead of the competition.

Additionally, our informative articles, tutorials, and resources are designed to help enhance your business website's performance and drive success. As a prestigious member of our affiliate program, you can earn extra money by referring our products to your contacts, benefiting from exclusive advertising materials, and dedicated support. By joining our affiliate program, you not only have the opportunity to earn extra money but also gain access to exclusive advertising materials and dedicated support. This will enable you to effectively promote our products to your contacts and maximize your earning potential. Earn free points by reading content, sharing links, and referring visitors to sign up for our website, which can be checked in the footer section. Moreover, you can redeem with cash.

In addition, our affiliate program offers a tiered commission structure, allowing you to earn even more as you refer more customers. This means that the more successful you are at promoting our products and bringing in new customers, the higher your earning potential becomes. So not only can you earn extra money through referrals, but you can also enjoy the benefits of a flexible and scalable income stream. Generate 10,000 points and redeem them. Read and generate points. Shop and generate points. Our publisher program gives you a link to share and generate points. Write and generate points. Whenever the reader reads, the author generates points. Imagine 10,000 people reading your article, and you generate 10,000 points. Affiliate program to generate 10% commission on every sale. Share your affiliate link. Smart move, to generate automated commissions.

In addition, our website also offers a user-friendly interface and a seamless browsing experience to ensure that you can easily access all the valuable resources and information. Furthermore, our customer support team is always available to assist you with any queries or concerns you may have, guaranteeing a smooth and hassle-free experience throughout your journey with us. Steps to success Register and update your profile.

Read daily to enhance your knowledge and generate points. Share your profile that you are now part of Media House with affiliate links on Face book, Twitter, LinkedIn, and others. So that whenever someone purchases anything, you can generate commission. You can check affiliate income 24 hours a day from your affiliate dashboard.

Share the news and articles with your affiliate link so that if sales occur, you generate the affiliate commission. Find problems of your near and dear and recommend our articles and books with your affiliate links. Read the publisher program page and share the links with your catchy lines. You can get a share of profit as points.

The content offers a strong call to action and effectively highlights the benefits of subscribing to the database and joining the affiliate program.

To improve it further:

1. Include specific examples of the valuable insights and skills available in the database.

2. Provide examples of exclusive advertising materials and dedicated support for affiliates.

3. Clarify how the free points system works and how they it can be redeem for cash.

4. Consider adding customers to

Understanding the points

Here, readers generate points by reading articles, sharing links from the publisher program page, and referring friends to sign up for the program. Customers can accumulate points by engaging with the platform in various ways. For instance, they can earn points by reading articles, sharing links from the publisher program page, and referring friends to sign up. These points can then be redeeming for cash or other rewards, providing an additional incentive for customers to active participate in the program.

This rewards system encourages customer engagement and loyalty. It creates a win-win situation for both the customers and the publisher.

For Author.

One of the main purposes of using Kal Mass Media for authors is to expand their reach and increase their visibility to a larger audience. By utilising the platform, authors can tap into a wide network of readers who are actively engaged in consuming content. This can lead to increased book sales, greater recognition, and potentially even opportunities for collaborations or partnerships with other industry professionals. Overall, Kal Mass Media provides authors with a valuable tool to promote their work and connect with their target audience on a larger scale.

Kal Mass Media is a platform where writers can share their expertise and contribute to the platform's knowledge. By joining the community, writers can highlight their skills and establish themselves as industry thought leaders. Kal Mass Media offers competitive compensation for writers, allowing them to turn their passion for writing into a sustainable income source. Whether you are looking for a side hustle or a full-time career, our platform provides the opportunity to turn your passion for writing into a sustainable source of income. Join now and build financial independence through writing on Kal Mass Media.

Kal Mass Media provides resources and strategies to enhance your online visibility, including keyword analysis and search engine optimization techniques. To enhance your search engine rankings and attract a wider audience to your reviews, you can utilize these methods. In light of the increasing significance of online reputation management, it is imperative to employ platforms like Kal Mass Media to establish oneself as a reliable and influential figure in one's respective domain. Kal Mass Media is designed to be search engine optimized for instant visibility on prominent search engines like Microsoft Bing, Seznam.cz, and Yandex.

Write to amaze others with your knowledge. Moreover, begin generating leads, selling your products, driving traffic to your videos (YouTube, Face book), and pressing the release button. A strong tools for display all your activities and reaches out the audience.

With one click, you can show all activities.

Writer's remuneration is also available for those who contribute high-quality content to our platform. We believe in rewarding our writers for their hard work and expertise. Earn competitive rates for your articles and tutorials, and gain recognition within our community. Start monetizing your writing skills today and join our team of talented contributors.

Do not miss this opportunity to display your talent and earn a steady income. Sign up now and start being paid for your valuable contributions. Here, writers can receive remuneration for every piece of feedback that is published. Select a product or vendor from the available categories: shopping, travel, literature, and Kbank.

Points Income: Points can be generated through activities like reading and writing content. In addition, whenever the reader reads the content, the author generates points. In addition, you can also generate points with the publisher programmer. A minimum of 10,000 points can be withdrawn. Only an active account can generate point income. No non-active accounts are eligible for this income.

Publish Income: Every time a writer creates content, it must be evaluated. Writers earn money once their work is approved and published. This can be found under his name on the right-hand side of the website's header and footer sections. This feature enables writers to simply track their earnings and growth. It promotes transparency and encourages writers to keep creating high quality content for the site. Moreover, whenever readers read the article, the writer earns points. Therefore, in this way, it is a win-win situation for authors.

Rewards: Additionally, the recognition that these awards provide can help them improve their professional reputation and create new opportunities in their respective industries. Furthermore, being able to demonstrate their published work and accompanying money can serve as a significant portfolio for writers looking for future possibilities in the field.

Each month, we will review the **best articles as reviewers, storytellers, and academics.** They will create rewards in this manner. Rewards are given in the form of rewards and recognition in this setting. Depending on the quality and impact of the articles, monetary rewards can range from cash prizes to gift cards.

For storytellers: As a storyteller, you can become an author at Kal Mass Media and have the opportunity to display your storytelling skills to a wide audience. By becoming an author, you can gain recognition and build a strong reputation in the industry, opening doors for future writing opportunities and collaborations.

Additionally, being part of Kal Mass Media allows you to connect with other talented storytellers and learn from their experiences, further enhancing your storytelling abilities. Moreover, start sharing your stories with a wide audience. By having your work published and recognized, you can establish yourself as a credible and talented storyteller, opening doors to potential book deals or collaborations with other writers or filmmakers. Additionally, being part of this platform allows you to connect with fellow storytellers, exchanging ideas and feedback that can further enhance your storytelling skills.

For students: Here, students can learn more by reading articles and eBooks. By becoming an author, a student opens the doors for many opportunities, such as getting their work published and reaching a wider audience. Moreover, the best part is that students can revise their lessons and improve their writing skills at their own pace. In this way, they can improve their knowledge of various subjects and become more well-rounded individuals.

In addition, open up the possibility for future opportunities and success with the Kal mass media points system. This system allows students to track their progress and receive recognition for their achievements.

This additional income source can help students meet their expenditures and reduce financial stress. By earning points through their work, students can also gain a sense of accomplishment and motivation to continue improving their skills.

Furthermore, the Kal mass media points system can provide students with a competitive edge in the job market, as employers often value individuals who have demonstrated dedication and success in their chosen field. Overall, this system not only benefits students academically but also prepares them for future professional endeavors.

For businesses, Kal Mass Media gives them a unique marketing system for their brands and boosts their sales. Additionally, the platform offers businesses valuable insights and analytics to optimize their marketing strategies. By utilizing the Kal mass media points system, businesses can effectively target their desired audience and increase brand visibility. This not only helps them attract new customers but also fosters customer loyalty and repeat business.

Moreover, the platform's analytics allow businesses to track the effectiveness of their marketing campaigns and make data-driven decisions for continuous improvement. Overall, Kal Mass Media serves as a valuable tool for businesses looking to enhance their marketing efforts and drive success in a competitive market.

By posting press releases and engaging with industry influencers, businesses can gain visibility and establish credibility in their target market. Moreover, Kal Mass Media gives friendliness to the search engines, which helps businesses improve their online presence and rank higher in search results. This increased visibility can lead to more organic traffic and potential customers discovering their products or services.

Additionally, Kal Mass Media offers various advertising options, such as sponsored content and banner ads, allowing businesses to reach a wider audience and generate leads. With its comprehensive suite of marketing solutions, Kal Mass Media empowers businesses to effectively promote their brand and attract loyal customers in today's digital landscape.

For Teachers: Kal Mass Media offers specialized tools and resources to engage students and enhance the learning experience. Teacher tools include interactive **quizzes**, **educational videos**, and **online forums** where students can collaborate and **discuss course** materials. By utilizing these resources, teachers can create a dynamic and interactive learning environment that caters to different learning styles and keeps students engaged. With Kal Mass Media's educational solutions, teachers can effectively deliver lessons and help students achieve academic success.

In addition to this, teachers generate their second income by engaging with and selling their own educational content or by offering tutoring services worldwide. With Kal Mass Media's educational solutions, teachers can effectively deliver lessons and help students achieve academic success. In addition to this, teachers generate their second income. There is one more tool here to understand, it is known as Library. It's give you additional income source.

For professionals: Here, professionals are advocates, doctors, engineers, and other individuals with specialized skills. By writing all about their skills and press releases, they can help them brand themselves and attract potential clients or employers.

In addition to this, they generate a second income with the Kal Mass Media platform. The Kal Mass Media platform allows them to monetize their expertise and reach a wider audience. In addition, as the readers read their content, they generate points, which can be used for various rewards and benefits offered by the platform.

For marketers: Always, marketers are looking for new clients or customers for their business. Kal mass media can provide a valuable platform to connect with potential customers and promote their products or services. Here, they not only engage clients for their target traffic but also have access to a wide range of advertising options and data analytics to optimise their marketing strategies.

Moreover, by becoming an author, they can establish themselves as thought leaders in their industry and gain credibility. Additionally, authors can also earn rewards and benefits through the Kal Mass Media Points System. As they publish content with Kal Mass Media, they start generating traffic to their target and accumulate points that can be redeemed for various perks and advantages.

For Journalist.

At Kal Mass Media, the Points System provides an additional incentive for journalists to actively contribute to and engage with the platform. And with the Kal Mass Media tools, they can generate more subscribers for their media house or publication. And more traffic for their YouTube channels. Ultimately, they will increase their online presence and revenue, contributing to the growth and success of their media career.

In addition, the Points System also fosters a sense of competition among journalists, motivating them to consistently produce high-quality content. This not only benefits their individual careers but also enhances the overall reputation and credibility of Kal Mass Media as a reliable source of news and information. With these added incentives, journalists are encouraged to go beyond in their reporting, resulting in a more vibrant and diverse media landscape.

Ebooks: Kal Mass Media is able to reach a wider audience and expand its influence in the digital realm. Kal Mass Media book store helps users gain more knowledge in the fields of **business, marketing, and health**, ultimately contributing to a more informed society.

In addition, the availability of eBooks also allows for greater accessibility and convenience for readers, as they can easily access and **download books** from **anywhere** and **at any time**. This further promotes a culture of continuous learning and personal growth within society.

Furthermore, by offering a diverse range of eBooks in various fields, Kal Mass Media caters to the diverse interests and needs of its audience, ensuring that there is something for everyone to benefit from. You can access the store at **https://kalmassmedia.com/book** store.

Furthermore, by offering a diverse range of eBooks in various fields, Kal Mass Media caters to the diverse interests and needs of its audience, ensuring that there is something for everyone to benefit from. Whether you are interested in self-help, fiction, or academic research, Kal Mass Media's extensive collection of ebooks has you covered. With just a few clicks, readers can explore new topics and expand their knowledge in the comfort of their own homes.

Create a free profile.

By creating a free profile on the website, users can easily save their favorite ebooks, track their reading progress, and receive personalized recommendations based on their interests. Additionally, Kal Mass Media regularly updates its collection with new releases and exclusive content, ensuring that there is always something fresh and exciting for readers to discover.

Whether you're a student looking for scholarly articles or a professional seeking the latest industry insights, Kal Mass Media's eBooks provide a convenient and comprehensive resource. With an easy-to-use interface and a vast array of subjects to choose from, readers can dive into their areas of interest and stay up-to-date with the latest research. Start exploring today and unlock a world of knowledge at your fingertips.

How to introduce yourself to the Society: Once you created your profile, and updated your photo and about us section. It is time to tell the world, that you are the affiliate of Kal Mass Media. Now, you can connect with like-minded individuals and share your passions and expertise. By joining online forums and communities, you can engage in meaningful discussions and establish connections with people who share similar interests.

Additionally, you can also contribute to the society by sharing valuable insights and knowledge through blog posts or articles on Mass Media's platform. In addition to this, you can share your affiliate link profile with others on social media platforms to expand your network and connect with even more like-minded individuals. So that whenever, someone clicks and reach the platform through your link, and generate sales, you can earn a commission or referral bonus. This can be a great way to monetize your online presence and earn passive income. It is a win-win situation for both parties involved.

Library revenue: Library revenue is the **lifetime royalty income** earned by content writers. The content writer can sell his article here and receive 30% of the default value of Rs.35. The writer must choose a library category to sell his work while composing. By selling their work in the library, writers can establish a passive income stream.

Writers can reach a larger audience and potentially make more money by categorizing their work appropriately. This not only encourages writers to generate good and marketable content, but it also allows them to diversify their income sources on the site. In addition, the library program provides writers with a platform to display their expertise and gain recognition within their chosen category.

This can lead to further opportunities for collaboration and increased exposure for their work. Additionally, the library revenue generated from content sales can serve as a stable source of income for writers, allowing them to focus more on their craft and continue producing high-quality content.

Furthermore, participating in the library program can also help writers build a loyal readership and establish themselves as authorities in their field. This can open doors to speaking engagements, book deals, and other lucrative opportunities outside of the site. Ultimately, the library program not only benefits writers financially but also helps them grow professionally and expand their reach in the writing industry.

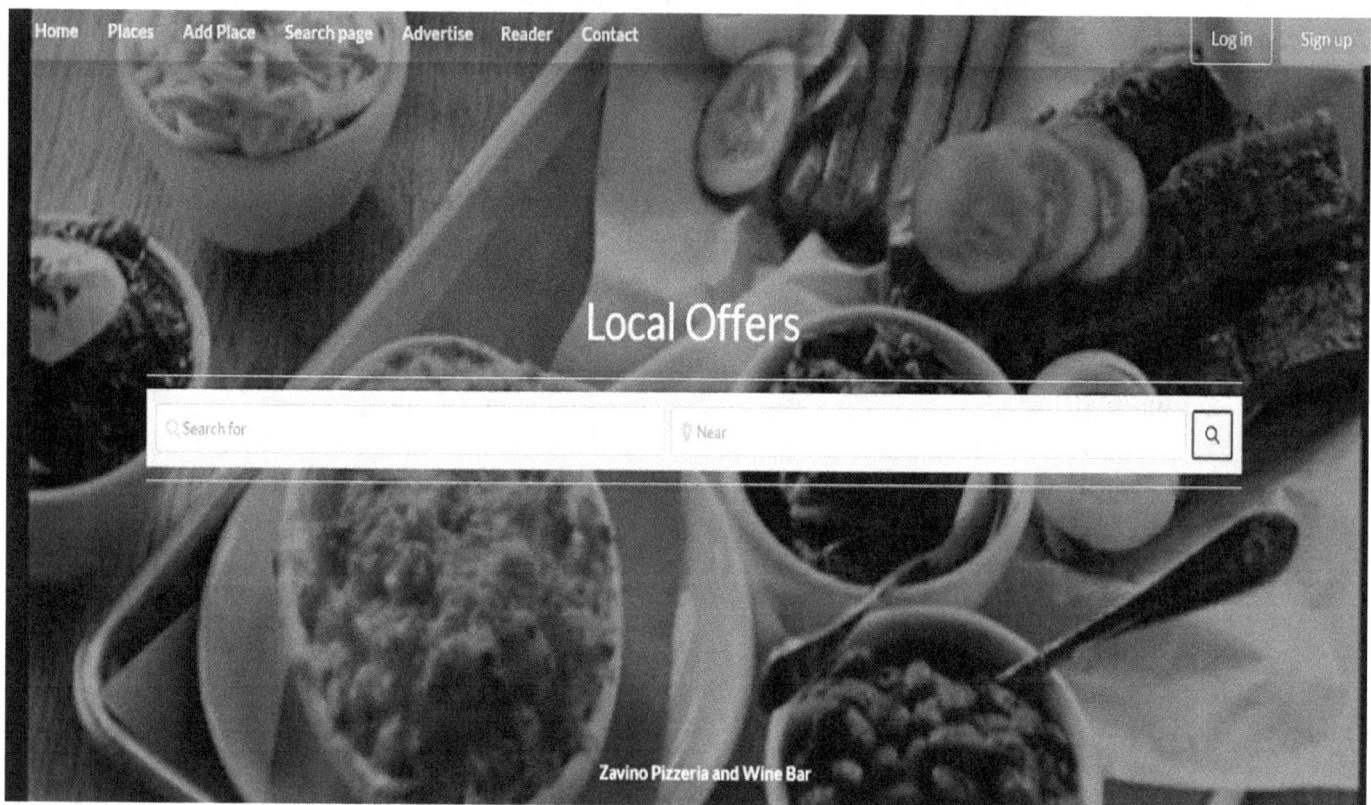

Shopping: Here you can explore your favorite merchant and start shopping your daily needs product. Shopping for your daily needs from Kal Mass Media shopping page not only provides convenience but also offers a wide variety of products to choose from different merchants. With a diverse range of merchants available on the Kal Mass Media shopping page, users can easily find products that cater to their specific needs and preferences.

Additionally, the platform's user-friendly interface and secure payment options ensure a seamless shopping experience for customers. Shop more to generate more shopping points and redeem exciting rewards and discounts on future purchases.

By regularly shopping on the Kal Mass Media shopping page, users can accumulate shopping points that can be used to unlock exclusive deals and promotions. Do not miss the opportunity to save money and enjoy a rewarding shopping experience by choosing Kal Mass Media as your go-to online merchant.

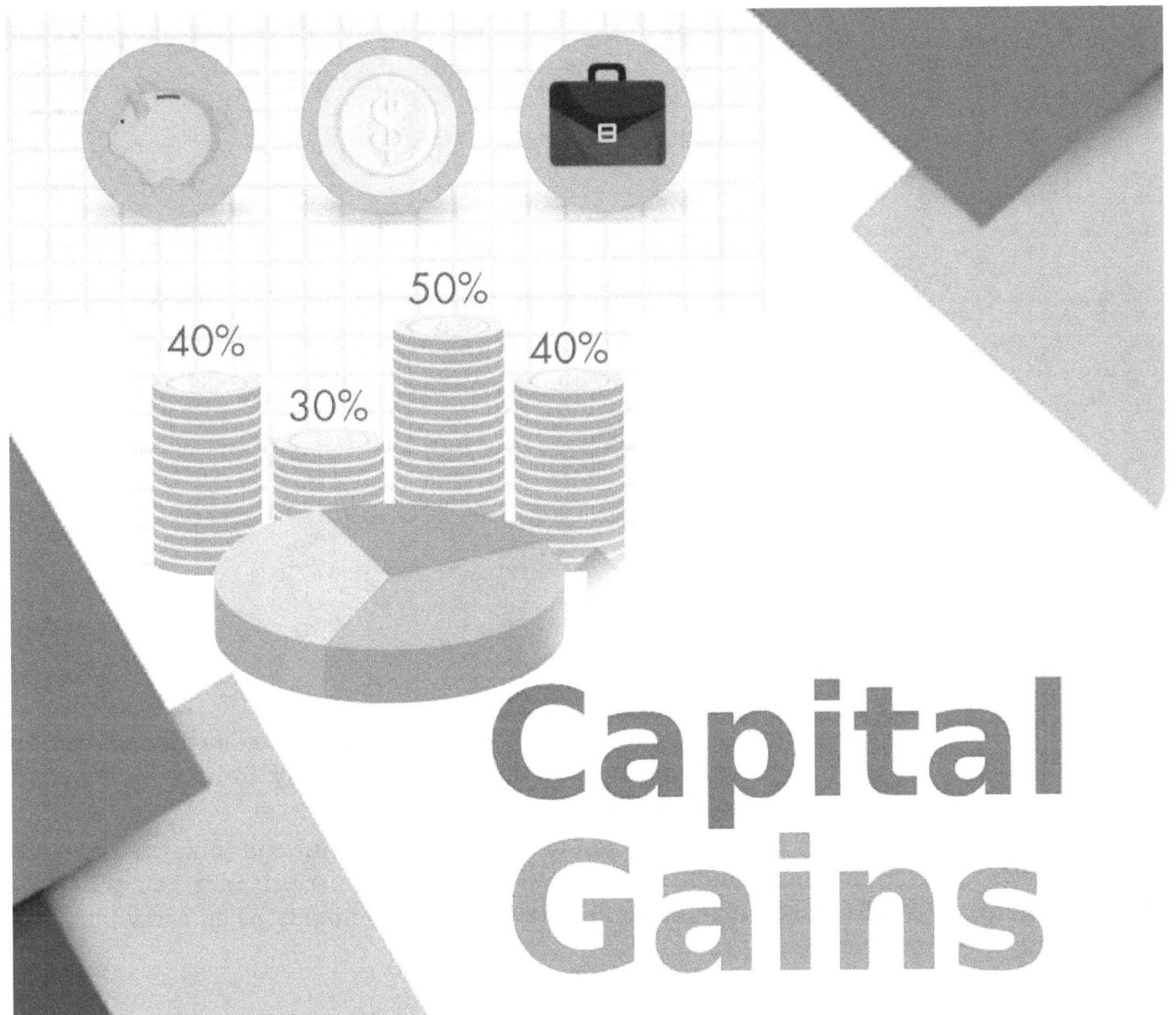

Capital Gains

Cash your points. You can redeem minimum 2000 points and the conversion rate will be updated to your wallet account. In addition, that amount can use for advertising anytime. Moreover, you can cash out your points for discounts on future purchases. You can accumulate 10000 points to receive in your bank account.

Affiliate income. In addition to earning shopping points, Kal Mass Media also offers the opportunity to generate affiliate income. By referring friends and family to shop on our platform, you can earn a percentage of their purchases as commission.

Start your savings and earning with Kal Mass Media affiliate program. At our affiliate dashboard, you can track your referral activity, commission earnings, and overall performance. You can create affiliate link for any Kalmassmedia.com pages and start earning commissions on every purchase made through your referrals.

Conclusion: Join our affiliate program and start earning money while helping your loved ones save. Do not miss this incredible opportunity to turn your network into a source of income. Sign up now and unlock the potential of affiliate marketing with Kal Mass Media! Kal mass media is for learner s of all levels, offering a wide range of educational resources and materials. By becoming an affiliate, you not only have the opportunity to earn money, but also contribute to the growth and success of individuals seeking knowledge. Join us today and be a part of our mission to empower learners worldwide!

BOOKS BY THIS AUTHOR

Shall I Trust

HOW WOULD WE KNOW IF SOMEONE IS COMMITTED OR NOT?

BOOKS BY THIS AUTHOR

Sell With The Ccc Formula

Sell your stuff with the CCC formula. Grow your sales and income. Learn once and apply it for the rest of your life